Community Helpers

Teachers

by Tami Deedrick

Content Consultant:
Philip Strittmatter
National Association
of Professional Educators

Bridgestone Books
an imprint of Capstone Press

Bridgestone Books are published by Capstone Press
151 Good Counsel Drive, P.O. Box 669, Mankato, Minnesota 56002
www.capstonepress.com

Library of Congress Cataloging-in-Publication Data
Deedrick, Tami.
    Teachers/by Tami Deedrick.
    p. cm.--(Community helpers)
    Includes bibliographical references and index.
    Summary: Explains the tools, schooling, and work of teachers.
    ISBN 1-56065-731-6 (hardcover)
    ISBN 0-7368-8032-1 (softcover)
    1. Teachers--Juvenile literature. 2. Teaching--Vocational guidance--Juvenile literature.
    [1. Teachers. 2. Occupations.] I. Title. II. Series: Community helpers (Mankato, Minn.)
LB1775.D384   1998
371.1'0023--dc21
                                            97-40282
                                              CIP
                                              AC

Editorial credits
Editor, Timothy Larson; cover design, Timothy Halldin; photo research, Michelle L.
  Norstad
Photo credits
Unicorn Stock Photos/Dennis MacDonald, 4; Joel Dexter, 6; Karen Holsinger Mullen, 8;
  Tom McCarthy, cover, 10; Jeff Greenberg, 12; A. Ramey I, 14; Robin Rudd, 16; Martin
  R. Jones, 18; MacDonald Photography, 20

3 4 5 6 7 8 11 10 09 08 07 06

Table of Contents

Teachers 5

What Teachers Do 7

Different Kinds of Teachers 9

Where Teachers Work 11

When Teachers Work 13

Tools Teachers Use 15

Teachers and School 17

People Who Help Teachers 19

How Teachers Help Others 21

Hands On: Teach a Friend 22

Words to Know 23

Read More 24

Internet Sites 24

Index 24

Teachers

Teachers help students learn new things. A student is a person who studies at a school. Teachers help students understand facts and ideas.

What Teachers Do

Teachers help students learn about subjects. Reading, writing, and art are subjects. Math and science are subjects. Teachers grade papers and tests. They take students on field trips. A field trip is a trip to see things and learn.

Different Kinds of Teachers

Some teachers teach many subjects. They teach reading, math, and science. Other teachers teach one subject like art or music. Some teachers teach students who need extra help.

Where Teachers Work

Teachers work at schools. Some teachers stay with one group of students all day. They teach in one classroom. Some teachers teach in more than one classroom. They teach many groups of students.

When Teachers Work

Teachers work during the school day. Sometimes they take work home at night. Teachers work during the school year. Some teachers teach summer school, too.

Tools Teachers Use

Teachers use learning tools. A learning tool is anything that helps people learn. Teachers use books and computers. They show movies. Teachers also use pictures, charts, and maps.

Teachers and School

People who want to be teachers must finish college. College is a school people go to after high school. Teachers also practice teaching in classrooms. They must pass special tests before they can teach.

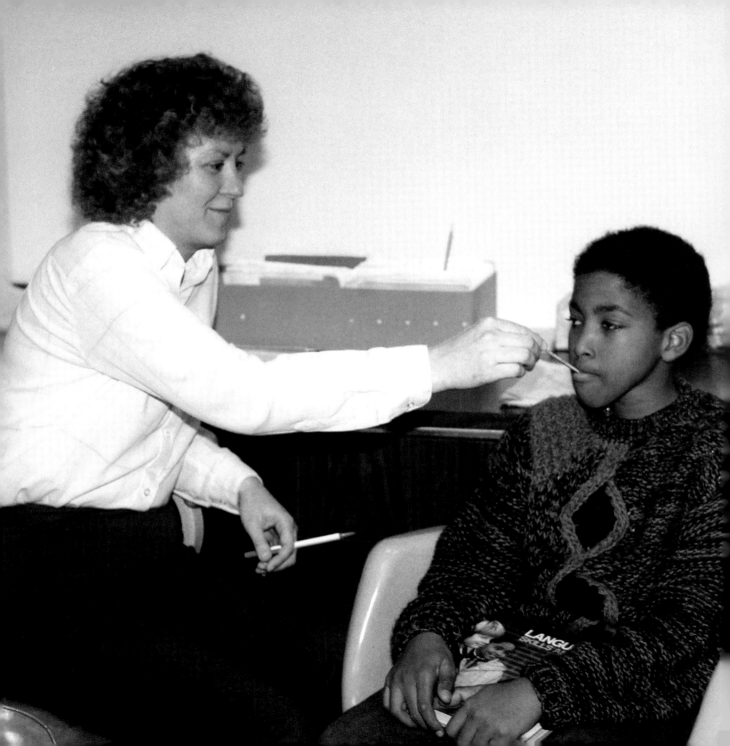

People Who Help Teachers

Principals help teachers make decisions. Teachers' aides help teachers teach students. School nurses help by taking care of sick students. Janitors help by keeping schools and classrooms clean.

How Teachers Help Others

Teachers help students learn about the world. They help students learn about communities, too. A community is a group of people living in the same area. Teachers also help students learn about each other.

Hands On: Teach a Friend

Teaching is a hard job. But it can also be fun. You can discover what it is like to be a teacher. Help a friend learn a magic trick.

What You Need

One book of magic tricks. You could try *Abracadabra* by Amy Jones.

What You Do

1. Read how to do one simple magic trick.
2. Practice each step until you know how to do the trick.
3. Show your friend each step of the trick.
4. Tell your friend how you do each step.
5. Have your friend practice each of the steps.
6. Give your friend hints on how to do the steps better.
7. Answer questions your friend may have.
8. Have your friend show you the trick.

Words to Know

college (KOL-ij)—a school people go to after high school

community (kuh-MYOO-nuh-tee)—a group of people living in the same area

field trip (FEELD TRIP)—a trip to see things and learn

learning tool (LURN-ing TOOL)—anything that helps people learn

student (STOO-duhnt)—a person who studies at a school

Read More

Cutlip, Glen W. and Robert J. Shockley. *Careers in Teaching*. New York: The Rosen Publishing Group, 1997.
Selden, Bernice. *The Story of Annie Sullivan: Helen Keller's Teacher*. Milwaukee: Gareth Stevens, 1997.

Internet Sites

FactHound offers a safe, fun way to find Internet sites related to this book.
Go to www.facthound.com
He'll fetch the best sites for you!

Index

art, 7, 9
books, 15
college, 17
computers, 15
facts, 5
field trip, 7
ideas, 5
janitors, 19
math, 7, 9

music, 9
papers, 7
principals, 19
reading, 7, 9
school nurses, 19
science, 7, 9
summer school, 13
teachers' aides, 19
tests, 7, 17